107

Mbella Sonne Dipoko · Black and white in love

MBELLA SONNE DIPOKO
POEMS

BLACK
& WHITE
in love

HEINEMANN
LONDON · IBADAN · NAIROBI

Heinemann Educational Books
48 Charles Street London W1X 8AH
P.M.B. 5205 Ibadan · P.O. BOX 25080 Nairobi

EDINBURGH · MELBOURNE · AUCKLAND
TORONTO · HONG KONG · SINGAPORE
NEW DELHI · KUALA LUMPUR

ISBN 0 435 90107 9

Printed in England by
Cox & Wyman Ltd, London, Reading and Fakenham

mikenge mi yabon na keke
ońola ndolo na konja

CONTENTS

AUTHOR'S Some of the poems included in this volume have already
NOTE appeared in *Transition*, *Présence Africaine*, and in the
anthologies *West African Verse* (Longmans, London),
Modern African Poetry and *African Writing Today*
(Penguin Books, London); *The Night*, *Progress* and
Two Girls were broadcast by the BBC. But I have
since had to recast most of them, changing a word
here and there, occasionally eliminating whole lines
and adding new ones, and often shortening some of
them considerably, as in the case of *Our Destiny* which
first appeared in *Transition*. I first wrote *My People*
and *Ten Years of Europe* (under another title) as
prose poems, which I have now shortened into verse
form. The title poem is being published for the first
time. However, what follows may be considered as the
definitive version of the poems. M.S.D.

BLACK AND WHITE IN LOVE
(*for B in San Francisco*)

There is a city in Yorkshire I will not name
I'll leave it to friends to whisper
The five letters which suggest
The eternity of metal
More than the metaphysics of love.
I remember it by the colour of autumn
And the laments of the winds on the moors
And me calling on you
In your room
Where, cross-legged,
You were yoga-ing the evening away
And all the after-holiday talk of Cuba
And of the beaches of Havana
Which I didn't know
And which those days only meant
Your girlfriend S whose lover I was
And because of whom we met
And my sadness when you left for Oslo
With only a few lines on you
To link your past and my past
With a future I hoped would be made
Of a lasting friendship.

Now, there's no need for you to feel jealous
Because of the scooter trip with S to Gosforth
The day you saw me in bed with her
And you left for Oslo
Although sometimes
Tears run down
Certain corners of my memory
Whenever I recall the beauty
Of the Cumbrian mountains
And of the Irish Sea at Seascale
And an old love on the rocks
Because of you and me.

[1]

Black and White Rydal Water
in Love Windermere
And Derwent Water
Were mirrors reflecting you
And your brown eyes
As we talked for the first time
Sitting by the fireplace
And the music on records was of a home
Just north of Zululand.

II We met again
But in Paris
With talk of trains
And talk of Turner
And of Norway
And the most yellow autumn in the world
And I had resumed my former job
Of a newspaper vendor
Which I used to do with S
While she was in Paris
And was living with me
Learning what it meant
To be poor
And a poet.

Like bums
S and I foraged for food in Les Halles
Filling our bags
With potatoes, vegetables
And fruits
Out of which she made jam
In jars supplied by Irma
My German-born landlady
To whom I still owe a lot of money
For unpaid rent.

[2]

Then S returned to London
Hitch-hiking from the Porte de la Chapelle,
In her handbag a ticket from her mother
For the channel-crossing,
And me waving bye-bye
Without as much love
As I have for you
As the DS was driving away with her.
I nevertheless played the guitar that night
Missing her
And singing
As she used to sing
A French folksong
Playing that same guitar
Before we went out foraging
In Les Halles.

From London
And just before she left
For South America
She sent me some money
And the key to that flat of hers
In the north of England
Where you and I were to meet
When a month later
She returned from Havana
And she met you in London
Newly-arrived from America
And brought you to Yorkshire
For a few days
And you and I fell in love.

I remember her
Asking me in bed
You love her,
Don't you?

[3]

Black and White And me only smiling
    in Love And her shaking her head.

My sadness with her began
At the beginning of my happiness
With you.

IV And now we are in the Paris of my eight years
The evening you arrived
A knap-sacked traveller on the horizon of my desire
And we are walking past Notre-Dame
On our way home in the Marais
And I am talking about tomorrow
With the simplicity of a child
Who can never have enough of the sweets of hope
A wind is coming up the Seine valley leading away the
        clouds
From near the stars and a haughty moon.
You are carrying my first present to you –
Red roses and in your heart you are pecking like a dove
At the words of love
While in my thoughts and because of the strain known
In our cruel world
Only to those who have ever loved
One who is not of their own colour
I am desperately wishing you were black
Because then, half the problems of prejudice would have
        vanished
Leaving only two human beings
To plot out their future
On the chart of fate.

V Still you and I had a lot in common –
Vegetarian obsessions
A passion for communicating
With the spirits

[4]

Black and White Accepting the ancients and the moderns,
in Love And a moving belief
In the Gods and the angels.
And there are times
I think with a smile
About the Scorpio lady
Of the Rue de la Huchette
And the rings
And time reminding us
That even in Paris
No neon light can beat
The splendours of a clear sky.

And then how we discovered each other
Naked as our ancestors were created
Before greed and fear caused some of them
To bequeath hate and all sorts of prejudices
To their after-days
Which were to become our days
Even after centuries of the prophets
And the divine call to love.

VI And I had that bicycle
S's present to me
On which she had arrived
To see me off
At Victoria Station
Where I took the train
To Folkestone
And then the ferry to France
Hurrying to be there
When you arrived
From Norway.

And you bought yourself a bicycle
In the rue de Rivoli

[5]

Black and White Because we had decided on Spain
in Love And some sun in the south.

VII We left Paris by train
With our bicycles and all
And crossed the frontier
Just after dawn
And wasn't it wonderful
To see again
An infinitely blue sky
And a very very blue sea?

VIII We arrived in Barcelona
Just before sunset
And left by another train
That same night
For Valencia
Where we ate oranges
Outside the station
Trying to make up our minds
About where next to go
Before deciding on Cullera
For which we left
In a railcar
The following morning,
Fat Spanish women interrupting their noise
In order to make the sign of the cross
At the first whistle of the train.
And then the sun
On the plains of Valencia
And the Sierra de Corbera
And sea-gulls sailing
Over the paddy fields of Sueca.

IX We took a flat near the beach
And from the balcony

[6]

Balck and White
in Love   I could almost count the waves
As they came kneeling down
On the shore.
We had the beach to ourselves
Most nights when we sat on the fine sands
And watched the dark waves heaving with the soothing
    winds
And above, gorgeous shooting stars in *fiestas* of tasselled
    light.
Fishing boats went out to sea
At dawn
Looking like buoys on fire
And they returned in the morning
Sailing up the Rio Júcar.

X The hard days also return
Glowing with a glory all their own
Revelling on the music of empty stomachs feeding on
    themselves.
But we did not panic when we got broke
Because I am a veteran of hunger
Although it wasn't easy at all in Spain
Not knowing anyone I could go to
For a little loan
And no place that we knew of
Where we could forage for food
As in the days of S.

And then we received that invoice
For the food we had ordered
From a vegetarian store in France
And for which I had sent a cheque for one hundred and
    eleven francs
Which they wanted supplemented by another thirty
    francs
Because the prices had risen with the Value Added Tax.

[7]

Black and White We thought the thirty francs quite a mess of money
in Love And decided I should write to them
Cancelling the order as well as the cheque
When the postman delivered to us that invoice
With the wonderful news that the food had arrived
And we could take immediate delivery of it
After paying the small postal charge of eighteen pesetas
Of which unfortunately we had only two
Being broke as we had never been broke together before.
And we were down to our very last matchstick.

We hitch-hiked to Valencia
To discuss with a French bank there
The telexing to me
Of all the money I had in France
(Just over a hundred francs!)
As we had been told by a bank clerk in Cullera
A few days before
That a new government order in Paris forbade
Drawing a cheque abroad on a French bank.
But the bank in Valencia had closed for the day
By the time we got there
And we had to return to Cullera
To be saved by the refund money
For the empty bottles we had in the house.
We got just enough
From the grocery store for them
To claim the food from the railway station
And buy a box of matches.
We had a feast of brown rice and soy sauce that evening
And a dessert of almond cookies
And at night made love
Like Olympic gold medallists
In top form.

XI And do you still remember

[8]

Black and White Our visit to the sanctuary up the hill?
in Love We stayed too long
Until someone got worried
And tactfully hustled us out
Talking of how *moderno* the little church was
Having been built near the ruins of a medieval castle
At the end of the last century.
We slotted views of the sea on telescopes
While the Franciscan friars who ran the place paced the
        precincts
Murmuring vespers to the saints.

XII And then the letter from Irma
Full of kindness
But also informing me
That she wished to sell
The bed-sitter in the Marais.
But as we had left the place in a mess
And I didn't want someone else
To put it in order for us,
We hitch-hiked
Back to France
Spending a whole wintry night
In a roadside café in Santa Susana
Listening to monotonous juke box music
Too broke even to buy a drink
While two Spanish couples played
A game of dice
And one of the men
Who was lean and sickly-looking
Like me
Drank mineral water
While the others were on cognac;
The lean man's wife flirting
With the other man
And I wondered

[9]

Black and White   About you and me
     in Love   If someday fate were to reduce me
To his condition
And you were still too hot
For compassion and abstinence;
What would happen then?
Me sitting there,
Lean and dying,
And you flirting with a friend of mine
And making fun of me?
For that woman did that as well,
Talking with mock care
To her husband
While winking at the other man
Whose wife got jealous.
I thought there would be a fight;
But the sickly husband only smiled –
Clearly one of those men
Who, although in contact
With the living,
Knew more about death
Than about life.

XIII   We left in the morning
By car
For Gerona
And then after the frontier
We were in France again –
Perpignan
Carcassonne
In the snow.

We nearly froze to death
Waiting for a lift
Just outside Toulouse.
It was a hard winter

[10]

Black and White And the message in the winds was hopeless
in Love Talking fiercely of the cold and landslides everywhere
In the West.
The rich and the well-fed went by in their cars
At top speed
As if rushing to hide their booty
From the rat-race of life in the West
Or as if hurrying to the scene of new plunders.
But the salvation which came in the guise of the big truck
Which finally gave us a lift
Wasn't without its own anxieties,
Was it?
What with that poor bird dying
On the windscreen
And me knowing what that meant
Even trying to pretend to myself I hadn't seen
What had just happened
And the apprehensive driver thoughtfully pronouncing it
A rare thing indeed
And you talking of a bird that died
On your windscreen
While you were driving home from work
In the States
And the subsequent death of your mother.
It was a bad omen
You said
Whenever a bird met with such an end to its days,
Which made our return to France
Very morbid indeed
As we counted dead cats and dogs
On the road to Bordeaux,
Where, after the truck driver had dropped us
At the port,
You caught a fever
While we were waiting
For the Dutchman sent to us by good fortune

[11]

Black and White To drive us right through to Paris
  in Love Where you became even more ill
And I did not like that at all
Because of the bird and the dead cats.
But everything was okay
After we saw a doctor
In the rue de la Montagne Sainte Genevieve;
And after putting the bed-sitter in order
And my books in paper boxes
I wrote an I.O.U. on a board
For Irma
Whose key we dropped in the letter box
And hitch-hiked to Versailles.
After a tour of the castle
And a short ride in a car
And an all-night lift in a truck,
We arrived in Limoges
Where we spent the whole of that day
Thumbing for a lift to the south.
There were no Good Samaritans out there that day
And I harangued you
On the hostility of your people
To the sight of a black man and a white woman.
And it was raining and snowing in turns.

In a brief lull
A monoplane took off with a man and woman
From a little aerodrome across the road
And I wondered if you envied her;
For there was a woman
Being taken to the skies by her man
When I couldn't even afford
A train ticket for you
After we got broke
Following that air trip you made with me
From Spain

[12]

Black and White To London
   in love So that we should not be apart
Even for those three days
I had to be away
For a pointless TV discussion.

XIV There was in London
An African girl I had left back home in Cameroon;
When she and I met in Belgravia
For the first time in ten years
She was disappointed
To find that I had become bearded
And shabbily-dressed
Wearing blue jeans
A tattered pair of shoes
I dragged along like slippers
And a waterproof coat
On the back of which I had painted
JAZZ
One of the magazines I used to sell.
And as if still not believing her eyes
She asked me if I had a car
And thought I was joking
When I said no
But I had an old sports bicycle
And when she did see it
She gave a derisive laugh
I will never forget
And when I asked of her second child
Whom she had told me and my parents was my child
She said I should forget about him.
Now that was a girl who had written to me
Over the past ten years or so
So many you-are-the-one-and-only-one love letters
That my disappointment with the materialism of modern
    love

Black and White   Was beyond words
in Love   When it occurred to me
Her tearful messages had been dictated
By the voice of social security
The adviser of every woman with a maternity bent of
    mind.
But I am such a dreamer and still believe
In the forgotten stories
Of man and woman together
For better or for worse.
That was why I locked you up in the bathroom
And beat the stars of pure romance
Back into her vision of the world
Missing the beginning of my affair with her in Tiko
When I was a young man aged twenty
Working as a clerk
In the accounts office
And earning less than ten pounds a month
And she was a nurse aged nineteen.
Her face still pops out of the windows of my mind
As it used to pop out of the windows of the hospital those
    days
To take a quick look at me while she was on night duty
And I was outside
Whistling a serenade
And waiting to take her home after her work.
I still remember the trains whistling past Ikange
Where she lived
And the moon making mirrors of dewy banana leaves
As we went home to the freedom of desire.

XV   The distant tomorrow felt very lonely indeed
On our way back from London
In spite of La Paloma just before take-off
And Winchester Cathedral in mid-air.
If only you were black

[14]

Black and White   I kept on saying to myself
in Love   If only you were black
Or at least red;
But white and bourgeois?
I loved you in the present
And hated you in the future
Fearing what you could become
In the ranks of our struggle –
If not exactly an outpost
Of the worst of your people
Who still oppress and exploit my people
At least a selfish voice
Always reminding me
Of the kids I've got to feed.
The snow on the mountains around Madrid
Made of life a small world of cold white sorrow.

You remember the return to Valencia
In a shower of rain
And the arrival back in Cullera
In a fog?
And then Irma's letter
And all the vexations of the trip to France?
And there we were now
In a nightmare of the bourgeois white world driving past
Indifferent to our plight in all that snow and rain.
You began to weaken in that rough weather
And I feared you might become ill
And I weakened too
Deciding on a criminal way out
By train to Perpignan
For which I signed a cheque you knew would bounce;
But it helped us leave Limoges that night
Arriving in Perpignan
Just as the sun was rising
Over the Mediterranean sea.

[15]

Black and White   We ate bread and cheese
in Love   In a park
And then hitched-hiked out of town.
The countryside was so bare
We couldn't find a decent hidden place to make love
On our way to La Junquera
And when the Police stopped us
We thought it was for the cheque.
But they only looked at our passports
And let us go.
France was only just recovering
From the abortive hopes of May
And Spain was in a state of emergency
Following the spread of the student revolt
To Iberian universities.
It was a dazzling, pearly afternoon
On the Costa Brava
After Figuras and the lift
By a real-estate manager.

XVI   Another lift
As far as Sitges
Just outside Barcelona
And then another
To that village
Where we hitched an evening train;
But when we told the ticket collector
We couldn't afford the fare to Tarragona
We were allowed without threats of prosecution to get off
At that station I will not name
Where we spent a warm night
As guests of nightwatchmen
Who talked communism
Waving an underground newspaper
Like a red flag.
We talked by the fireside

[16]

Black and White In a railway shed
in Love And they had that dog
That seemed to be listening
And you fell asleep
And they said I too could sleep and have some rest
Which I wouldn't do.
We left very early the following morning
And it was still dark
And very cold.
But the sun was soon rising
By the time we got to the main road
Just before the level-crossing.
Then one lift after another
And we were in Valencia again;
Too tired to continue on the road
You said couldn't we take the train
To Cullera?
I couldn't protest
Seeing the state in which you were
And so we had to use our last pesetas
For rail tickets
Expecting we'd meet some money for me
At the bank.
Nada hoy
Nothing today
Said the bank clerk
The following day.
Nada hoy
The next day
And the next –
Nothing from London
For the TV discussion
And nothing from Colorado
For the article
On African writing.
We owed money for the gas

[17]

Black and White And we had nothing to eat;
in Love So we hitch-hiked to Benidorm
Some sixty kilometres away
Where, at the filling station, we hawked
What books we had left,
A woman in a long car buying *Justine* for sixty pesetas
And at night I read poetry
For a bit of money
In the café *El Cid*
Before hitch-hiking back to Cullera
Just after mid-night
To arrive in the early hours of the morning
Glad that we would be able to pay for the gas
And have a few pesetas left for bread and cheese
And all the time we were involved with the black arts
Often fortune-telling by numbers
Sometimes by cards
And I saw the ghost of a friend long dead
And I was taught without words
How to dismiss those of the other world.
I am strange even to myself
With me equally treasuring
The grimoires and Marx and Mao.

XVII And when your spirits came through
You were afraid for my life;
But they were wrong about me dying
On the fourth of December
Which met me in Tangier
After I had quarrelled with D
Who having lent me some money
Because I was starving
Wanted me to consider him
As a father or some kind of imperial benefactor
And not as an equal
Who had been lucky to have grown fat

[18]

Black and White On the honey of my land
    in Love Sleeping with my sisters
            Down there in the south and south-east
            And returning to the edge of the desert
            Where I met him with so many souvenirs of his safari
            Across the kindness of my black people.
            On the day the spirits had said in Cullera I was going to
                die
            I sat alone in Tangier
            Burning candles and incense
            Renewing my link of life
            With the Most High
            Who alone can shuffle the stars of predestination
            And the following day
            Feeling better
            My hand in the hand of God
            I thought of you and I and the sierras and the sunsets.

    XVIII My diary says of one of those Spanish days:
            Misty in the morning
            Then the sun glows through the clouds
            And the sea is fringed in brown, green towards the
                horizon
            And the winds are full and cold and whine about Spring.
            Towards the night
            The dusk is blue
            Especially on the sierras
            Behind which the rosiness of the sun is paling away
            In splashes of violet and grey;

            The sea is brown
            Towards the shore
            Muddied by the waters of the Júcar,
            Dark beyond,
            And the orange floodlights
            Of the sanctuary and the castle

            [19]

Black and White On the hill
in Love Are on.
But *El Galeon* is still not lit up;
I wonder why
And the winds are still talking
Of the sea of spring.

I have decided
After Cullera
We shall be heading south
Probably staying a month or so
At Loja
Thus being near Malaga, Cordoba and Granada,
Depending on where
We find something cheap.

XIX Then when I thought
I had begun to love you
More than I had loved
Any other girlfriend
White or black
Before you
I decided it was time you left
For I knew I was about to enter
The most difficult period in my life
And I wanted to suffer alone.

I talked of sending you to Sweden
Where we had mutual friends
And where you could wait for me
While I consulted
With the keepers of solitude –
The oracle of the poets;
And you wept
And I wept when you weren't looking;
We loved each other so!

[20]

Black and White Then I changed my mind again
      in Love And thought you had better return
        XX To America.

We discussed your departure
Riding our bicycles
At dusk
From El Perello
And old Spanish peasants
(Riding mule-drawn carriages
Under which their dogs walked
Between the wheels)
Were returning home
After an afternoon of work
On the rice fields of Sueca
Or in the orange groves.
The wind was coming
From the Albufera
To play with your long hair
And it was easier to cry then,
Hiding tears in the night.

XXI And do you still remember how
In the shadows of the sierras
I used to talk to you
Of the glory of the struggle
For national liberation
And you just sitting there
And it not occurring to you
What a fool I was
Spending my time
Making love
In the underground
And fighting my revolutions
In the head?

Black and White   Darling,
    in Love   We were drunk of each other
And even more so
When, some four months
After our arrival in Spain
We left Cullera at sunset,
Bicycling to Malaga
On your way back
To San Francisco.
The breath of the night
Was of orange blossoms
And stars shone
Over Alicante
Far away
And we slept in the open
Under olive groves.

XXII   Dear B,
You are the only other one who knows
About that night
At the building lot
In Cartagena
And the following night
On the way to Mazarron –
All the dogs barking
And the mules and the horses neighing
And strange birds crying
And you and I exhausted,
Trying to have some sleep
On the dew-drenched shoulder
Of the Sierra de la Almenara
And the Guardia Civil looking for us
Riding on their snorting motorbikes!

What of the clouds
And the mirage of a sea

[22]

Black and White In the light-streaked horizon
in Love Over mountain passes?

The following morning
We were on the road again
Battling with the same mountains
And then, just after mid-day,
We arrived on the waterfront
In Mazarron where we had siesta
On the verandah of an unlived in villa
Facing a windy sea.

XXIII Aguilas later that evening
Where we spent the night
On a beach just outside town
And you cooked our little dinner of brown rice
Miso and *soy* sauce
Under a big moon
While I was singing
To the winds
Good old Tennyson's
Sweet and low
Sweet and low
Wind of the Western Sea . . .

XXIV Then because we had no money left
And only your air ticket,
We sold our bicycles
At an hotel
And hitch-hiked to Cuevas
And then to that little village
Where we caught a bus
To Almeria.

XXV Let the other place names ring
In your memory:

[23]

Black and White Sierra de Nevada,
in Love Motril,
And then of course,
Nerja,
That little town,
All white and blue
And so clean
Against the mountainside!

XXVI It wasn't easy
Finding a place
To spend the night
In Almeria
Because, as the hoteliers said,
We weren't *matrimonio*.

But we finally found a room
And two days later
We were in a bus again
And then at the airport
In Malaga
Our kisses
And talk of Tangier
Our kisses
I say
And the embraces
In the sadness of goodbye
All very painful
After a love affair lasting over six months
Through the north of England,
France in the autumn and winter
And Spain in the winter and Spring.

Did you see me still waving
Even after your plane was air-borne?

Black and White I saw your Piscean palm
in Love Against the glass window
And I recalled the divine numbers
Of our nights of the Kabalah.

    XXVII I bummed around for days
Half-starving after you had left.
Torremolinos
Fuengirola
Marbella
Estepona
Sleeping on the beaches
And typing stories at dawn
Sitting on beach chairs
Before the arrival of the sun-bathers.

Sometimes at night
The *Policia* flashing torches
Demanded to see my *pasaporte*
And I showed it to them
And they asked
De donde viene?
And I told them
From where I was coming
And then:
A donde va?
And I told them
I was going to Algeciras
Where, because of the one-way visa
I got in Valencia,
Remember?
Très meses
They wouldn't let me go
And work as a labourer
In Gibraltar
And so I had to return

Black and White To Fuengirola
in Love Where I got some second hand books
From a kind book-selling Englishman
And I sold them for a commission
In the streets of Torremolinos
Before returning
To Algeciras
From where I ferried
To Tangier
Where on my first night
In the free port,
And having taken them off
In order to sleep
On the sands of Malabata Bay
An Arab boy stole
My only pair of shoes
And I had to walk bare-footed
Feeling even closer
To the visiting hippies
On the heights of grass.

XXVIII On my third day
In Tangier
I went to the Post Office
And was given a parcel
Of twelve complimentary copies of my first novel
A Few Nights and Days
From one of my publishers in London
And some money from you
With a letter saying
You thought I would need it;
And indeed I needed that bread,
Baby, for as usual,
I had arrived stone broke,
And the copies of the novel
I hawked in the streets.

[26]

Then Heinemanns cabled me some money
And before I was broke again
I bought some nice Moroccan things for you
For which I was later unable to afford
The very small postage
And I had to pawn
Those nice Moroccan things
And I pawned even my Holy Bible
For bread
Just to stay alive
And give thanks to God
For our love.

January-February 1971

OUR Anthems and flags
DESTINY Medals of gold . . .
Say, witness of our suffering,
Who are these innovators,
Inheritors of former kingdoms?

But the night will not reply
Pre-occupied with tomorrow
Living the centuries
Not knowing the years.

II And we sang our memory
Ritual rags lacquered with blood
In the naked ways of the night
Obeying an incarnate instinct
To link the real with the unknown
Multiform in the universe.

III We are the progeny of a great heritage
We are the progeny of an infinite past
Naked in love and in hatred naked
Creating in blood and dying in blood
Crimson blossoms of shattered virginity
Bleeding wound in the Amazon's heart
Bleeding wound in the warrior's breast
And behind
In the villages and towns
The sinewy lines of the mind's creation
The order of the ruler and the ruled
Served by the throaty voice of drums,
Served by the thoughtful, less buoyant music of strings
And all the time
God of the gods
Creating the glory of masks
Laying the landmarks of the spirit.

[28]

Our Destiny We are the moderns in time
    IV Groping after tomorrow
        Shying away from the naked kingdoms of history
        Trying to build new cities
        In a world of clean flags
        Which is not progress
        The causes remain the same
        The rituals have only gone into trenches
        And sacrificial blood flows in pipe-lines.
        Things are being done in secret which were done in
            public;
        We become like all mankind
        Decent without
        Indecent within
        Scaling the years on the backs of others.

    V We lose our authenticity in its quest
        And to thinkers more than three times in the morning
        And to thinkers more than three times in the evening.

        I opt for something else
        Not for the naked city;

        But make its glories eternal
        While our thoughts like travellers overtake our hesitations
        Heading for the distant tomorrow
        Cultivating out memory
        Creating the unknown
        Remembering without aping
        Our great grand parents in the valley of drums and rivers
        Our great grand parents in the dance of blood.

    VI Not for their ears
        The story of growth
        Not for their eyes
        The becoming.

        [29]

Our Destiny   Deaf in the depth of departure
Dumb in death.

Not for their joy
The new colours.

And the elephants lumbered in
Bulldozing the graves away
So do the mortal mighty of an affluent breed despoil
The monuments of departure
Leaving behind egocentric tracks of vanity.

VII   Never again will it rise
The old flag
Artificial rainbow that dried the sky of rain
Pompous drunkard draped in wind-borne colours.

And the oppressed freed themselves
And the oppressors killed themselves.

Glory of our struggle
Dressed in the uniform of hope.

1963

TO PRE-COLONIAL AFRICA And the waves arrived
Swimming in like hump-backed divers
With their finds from far-away seas.

Their lustre gave the illusion of pearls
As shorewards they shoved up mighty canoes
That looked like the carcass of drifting whales;

And our sight misled us
When the sun's glint on the spear's blade
Passed for lightning
And the gunfire of conquest
The thunderbolt that razed the forest.

So did our days change their attire
From hides of leopard skin
To prints of false lions
That fall in tatters
Like the wings of whipped butterflies.

1963

[31]

PAIN All was quiet in this park
Until the wind, like a gasping messenger, announced
The tyrant's coming
Then did the branches talk in agony.

You remember that raging storm?

In their fear despairing flowers nevertheless held
Bouquets to the grim king;
Meteors were the tassels of his crown
While like branches that only spoke when the storm
    menaced
We cried in agony as we fell
Slashed by the cold blade of an invisible sword.

Mutilated, our limbs were swept away by the rain;
But not our blood;
Indelible, it stuck on the walls
Like wild gum on tree-trunks.

1963

AUTO-BIOGRAPHY   We crawled and cried and laughed
Without hope
Without despair.
We grew up
Fenced in by the forest.
But this world of uncles and fathers and mothers and others
Our fine world of greenness and grins was blown away
By the terrible storm of growth
And the mind soon flung pebbles at the cranes of the off-shore island.

But today
Floods flee the rising sun
And owls hoot from the edge of the dark song.
Like cripples blinded by sandy winds
Dreams drift under the low sky of our sleep
And our hearts listen to the voice of days in flight
Our thoughts dusting the past.

1963

PROGRESS Sing marrowless creatures
the song of birds soaring high
you are a whole age
pompous livery of empty bones
that lure my eyes towards a home in space
while memory
like a reluctant child
shuffles away from the riverside
where love and marrow hold in anchor
my own and others of ancient stock.

Today I live among the birds
in the soulless kingdom of feathers
maybe tomorrow I too will begin to lose my marrow
in the nascent tribe of planes and rockets
while growing wings for the journey back home
where love and marrow hold in anchor
my own and others of ancient stock.

Listen,
it is for you I sing
you childhood by the far-away river
under the roaring of things in flight.

1961

A POEM OF   I am tempted to think of you
VILLENEUVE Now that I have grown old
ST. GEORGES And date my sadness
for M-C To the madness of your love.

All those flowers you hung
On my gate
All those flowers the wind blew
On the snow!
Why must I remember them now
And recall you calling me
Like a screech-owl
While I watched you
Through the window-pane
And the moon was over the Seine
And Africa was far away
And you were calling
And then crying
In the snow of exile
And the neighbour's dog barking as if bored
By the excesses of your tenderness?

When I came down for you
And opened the gate
Cursing the cold of your land
You always went and stood
Under the poplars of the river Yerres
At the bottom of the garden
Silently watching its Seine-bound waters;
And the moon might take to the clouds
Casting a vast shadow
That sometimes seemed to reach our hearts.

And then following me upstairs
You stopped a while on the balcony
As high as which the vines of the garden grew

[35]

A Poem of With those grapes which had survived
Villeneuve The end of the summer.
St. Georges You picked a few grapes
Which we ate.
I remember their taste
Which was that of our kisses.

And then in the room
You in such a hurry to undress
And you always brought
A white and a black candle which you lit.
Their flames were the same colour
Of the fire glowing in the grate
And you were no longer white
You were brown
By the light of the fires of love
At midnight
Years ago.

January 1971

[36]

ANOTHER Where is he
CHILD Our child
for H The link
In flesh, bone and blood
Of our love?

We caressed him
Caressing each other
We kissed him
Kissing each other
And we felt him moving
In your belly inflated with love;

Where is he
The little one
We saw growing up so fast
In our dreams?

When, upon the advice of your parents
You disappeared in the eighth month
Some talked to me of a foster home
And I have since been searching for our child
But have found only his absence
And your silence
And echoes of threats from your father
Who swore he would shoot two bullets into my waist
And who asked you to choose
Between him and me
And you chose the bank and the stock exchange
Rather than me and your child
And nights out in the open.

January 1971

[37]

LOVE Let's go and learn by the candles of fireflies
The difficult lesson on radio signalling
Which others older than us have left
On the blackboard of the long night
So that tomorrow when we are apart
We may transmit on the frequency of our love
Those intimate messages we can never post

II And the voice became silent
The night passed
Six times at eight o'clock
Twelve times the postman
Without a word for me.
Still from dawn I watched for the mail
I watched for the message dusk might bring.
Like a maimed dove the wind arrived with the perfume of
  time
Pining in the grottoes of our dreams
And the elected in the Night's kingdom prayed:
Eulogies to the initiated one!
And the tongues of the temple candles trembled
Lighting up the dream pages of love.

III Wipe your tears in the distance
I do not want to live any longer
For days have grown beards
And nights have become lonesome.
Letters cannot comfort me.
They remind me of the past which you know is dead
And so you send a ghost to me when you write those letters
Letting my lips kiss a face so far behind.

1963

[38]

THE NIGHT Today we are sitting
On the banks of another river
Sitting there and doubting whether or not
The golden river exists.
Our feet are in the water
Its cool smoothness soothes us
While a reed bends and sighs
Leaning against another reed
Like young people in love.

And our river becomes a cat black sad
Its flanks against our bare ankles
Our river becomes our night dark lithe
Moving by
At the pace of blind-folded time.

And you say
We are waiting
For the alarm clock
Complaining drowsily
And you say
We are waiting
For the clockbird
That capers
On wet leaves.

We are not waiting
For the alarm clock
Which will ring no more
Its spring being cut
And someone has played the clockbird's dirge
It lies dead
Under the window
Where blood-stained feathers will soon be made into a
    pillow
(But not by us)

[39]

The Night For another assailant's head
Snoring but killing in sleep.

True, the river's smooth body kills
Drowning us
And cat's paws drag the unfortunate
Into tiny streams of blood,
Which may be the truth.
But where are those streams of blood?
They must be near our dreams
From which we look
At another world
Even though the soothsayer spoke
As if the lines on our palms were rows of grain sown
In a field we plough with every step we take;
(In autobiography we reap
Searching in the fields of our past days)

And you say
We are waiting
For the alarm clock
Complaining drowsily
And you say
We are waiting
For the clockbird
That capers
On wet leaves.

1963

[40]

TO MY MOTHER

Between you and me also
There is a tenderness stronger
Than a mere affair of kisses
For by you I was born to a lion
Although I now look
More wretched than a duiker that has survived
The hunter's gun
And poisonous herbs.

My lioness
If I should ever get back home
Under our double star
You will cry at the sight
Of the wounds I have sustained
In my struggle
To keep my soul whole.

January 1971

PERSECUTION Why do I feel
The capitalist world is out
To get me?

Why do I feel
My mouth has become
A test tube
Of all the poisons
In the world?

Why do I feel
So lonely?

It is because I chose
The shooting stars
And the freedom
Of the open.

It is because
I am black
And a hippy
And I sing
The glory
Of my people
And the best friends are the gods
And the angels
And they are far away;
And although a hippy
I keep away
From dope and grass
And so can never
Get high enough
Where one can forget
All about the bloody reign
Of gold
In which the poet is an outlaw

[42]

Persecution To be murdered for daring
To trace a path
To the stars
In the human soul.

January 1971

ON GOD No revelation has come near
To the whole truth of your beginnings
In the imagination of man;
No fortune-teller knows of your end
And many scoff at your very existence
What kind of a parent are you then
Who cannot force your reality
On your children
While mothers of the world weep
Their little ones of the graveyards of hunger
And young girls lament their lovers
Sacrificed on the fronts of conquest?
You must strike hard,
You of the skies and signs,
You must strike hard
The oppressors of my people
As we liberate our lands with guns
Under the covering fire of your thunders
From beyond the orb of the horizon.

January-February 1971

[44]

MY PEOPLE   My people are in the villages all over Africa
             Tillers of the soil, fishermen of the rivers and the seas,
             Nomads wandering about with their cattle;
             The medicine man and his patients
             And the newly-born;
             Man and woman and boy and girl
             And all the children growing up
             And the old reaching unwillingly, painfully
             For the grave.
             The harvest is often meagre,
             The catch scanty
             And nomads are harassed on pasture lands
             By conflicting boundary claims.
             The sorcerers are losing their clients
             To the diseases of the cities
             And the mirages of false booms in which everything
                 costs money
             And the highly-educated are annexed to theories
             Far removed from the practice of patriotic courage.
             They too are my people –
             The university graduate selling his soul for a grant
             Or for a higher degree,
             The civil servant informing on his colleague
             In order to keep his post
             Or to secure a higher one
             And the policeman doing his job
             And sometimes overdoing it
             And the soldier of the state army
             And the revolutionary
             Who is the mortal enemy of capitalist tyranny
             And is the target of the regular soldier's gun.
             The ministers and the presidents
             Of one African republic or the other;
             They too are my people –
             Those whose souls are still whole
             And the corrupt

             [45]

My People　The patriots
And the traitors.
As a writer I cannot disown anyone.
I speak to all
Hoping that what I have to say will heal
Those souls which have been broken
And there are more broken souls among the *élite*
Than among the people who are protected
By the modesty of their material needs
And their distance from the journeymen of hate
Who, without realizing it, fear man more than God
And yet are too weak or too perverse
To be partisans of love
Beyond class and colourbar.

My people,
One is bound to feel alone
And to despair
In the face of all the horrible odds.
So send word of hope
From your hidden camps of victory
Or even from your prisons of defeat
That you are still dreaming
The beautiful ancient dream of freedom
And that we can start again
To put together the broken pieces of our plans
For the future.
My people,
One is bound to feel alone
In a time of cynical smiles and silences.

II You are of the villages
And you are of the rivers
And of the hillsides
And the valleys
And even of the mountains

[46]

My People And the deserts.
Some of your sorcerers are out of business
For they lost faith in themselves
And the bells of the foreigner's church rang just for that –
That we may lose faith in ourselves
And become hangers on of another culture.
But those who feel the stars
And know beyond the knowledge of interested opinion
    reassure us,
Their voices relayed to the temples of our hearts,
That all is not lost
And so there is no need to despair
For Africa will be free
And nothing will stop us from being free . . .

III I will go on talking of freedom
And of goodness
Even though the capitalist enemy is plotting our death
At every street corner
And across frontiers.

What does it matter
If some of us be murdered,
If we are thrown into jail
For the flimsiest excuses
Or if we should be consigned to the firing squad
Because we dared speak up
For our people?
Tomorrow will tell our children
That there were those among us
Who were never intimidated into submission;
That there were those among us
Who remained proud throughout the struggle
And accepted neither a fattening compromise
Nor the material security of a cynical partnership
With the oppressor.

[47]

My People And in their turn
Our children will be proud of our sacrifices;
They will be proud of our courage.
Armed with that memory
It would be easier for them to maintain their integrity
In the face of trials similar to the ones with which we are
    battling today.
These things matter in the writing of the history of a
    people
If it is to have echoes of glory.

IV Now, the villagers and the nomads and the small traders,
As well as the fishermen who play our rivers and our
    seas
Haven't got the same problems which beset
The African intellectual
And the city civil servant
And the Police Inspector
And the army officer
And the up-country administrator
Whose memories and imaginations are clogged
With the contagion of the worst of the West
And the contradictions of their academic exile,
Hence the phenomenon of acculturation
With its inbred mechanism of hypocrisy
Which makes the intellectual
In spite of his cultural nationalism
To be just as West-oriented
As his elementary-school educated son and daughter
Who look at the city with its individualism as the only
    desirable world
Of tomorrow,
All because those who direct them lack themselves
Any original direction from within their minds
And they say one thing and do another
Making of wishful thinking a treachery

[48]

My People They consider as academic brilliance.
And the people do not talk of socialism
Even though that is precisely what they need
For their integrity.
And drifting to the cities
Girls become prostitutes almost overnight
Making of their beautiful bodies
The supply and demand curves of desire.

Who will preach to my people
As they buy tickets to the traps of the human soul
It is for the *élite* to do the talking
Because of the knowledge they have gained
Of acculturation, and to guide.
But what kind of a message would it be
And in which direction will the people be led
If the leaders themselves have been corrupted
And have sold themselves out to the oppressors
For personal gain and frivolous honours?

Let us as Africans
Define an African sanctity
A purity by which to live
And die
For the love of our people
Who are asking to be led
Towards a better future.

So, you old woman
And the girl
Living alone
In village huts;
You old widower
And the widow of the man
Who did not return from the war

[49]

My People   Tell the policeman
When he raps a rough knock on your door
At dawn
That those who teach a people fear
Render the whole country defenceless;
For cowards are never good with guns
Not even when the foreign invader crosses the national
frontiers
And the armed forces are outflanked
And the state is menaced
And the government calls the people to arms.
Courage is born only out of the love and practice of
freedom.
Tell the policeman to go away
For you were born loving your country
And you have no time for civic lessons given at gun-point.

But I will not disown
Even the policeman who slaps the widow
And hits the widower's chest with the butt of a gun
Or who rapes the defenceless virgin of the village dawn
For although I deplore his crime
And grieve over the depravity of his soul
He nevertheless remains
One of my people
Just like all the others –
Honest tillers of the soil, fishermen of the rivers and the
seas,
Nomads of the hills and the valleys
And the glorious rebel redeeming the honour of his people
Gun in hand.

I will not disown
Even the scared presidents
Because of whose security

[50]

My People Armed guards go terrorizing the people
Even though I approve only of the socialist revolutionary
Who fights for a better day.

February 1970–February 1971

Let us all be poets
Declaring certain places regional capitals of poetry
And choosing a world capital of poetry
Where we could meet to poetize on the affairs of the world
And relaunch those best dreams of mankind
Which the politicians have betrayed.
These capitals should be out in the country
Where there are hills and valleys
Where there are streams or lakes
So that we may all be reminded of the beginning of time
And of the purity of the first days.
Annual assemblies will be held in the open
The first meeting under a full moon
All the debates, resolutions, minutes, and decisions in
    poems.
We shall assemble regardless of race
We shall be egalitarians
We shall be socialists
Concluding the first meeting with the dimming moon and
    stars
And sleep through the morning
Rising at noon for the next debates.
We shall be opposed to exploitation
Of one race by another
Of one individual by another
Of one country by another.
In this way we shall make of the exercise of power
A sublime affair of tenderness
Mobilizing every conscience for the task of human
    liberation
And the co-operation of peoples
Across the face of the earth.

December 1970–March 1971

[52]

TWO GIRLS Your loin-cloth is too small
Too small to cover those curves oiled and glistening
Like ebony exhibited at the National Museum.
As with your mouth you blow that fire
I think of the blacksmith with his pair of bellows
I think of the tinker hammering shapes into iron.

Ewudu, leave me alone
My place is here and I'm happy.

Ndongo, the city will demand your charms
And pay so dearly too
You will buy the finest dresses
And look like a flower kept by God
And the men of the city will come to you
And offer to buy your caresses
And pay so dearly too.

There is nothing in what you say to tempt my steps;
I'll stay where I am and blow this fire
And do as grandmother did before our mother now lying
          dead
Under those plantain leaves.

You stay here wasting your youth away
Under these bewitched bushes
While in the city life flows
In stream-like streets.
There is enough for all to drink
Enough for all pretty girls
For beauty is a cup with which to draw the water of life.

Ewudu, leave me alone
I have this fire to blow
And fields to hoe tomorrow

[53]

Two Girls Lobsters by the riverside
Mushrooms at dawn.

The men of the city are inviting me
To sleep with them in netted beds
Which protect one against mosquito bites;
Listen! One has just passed, saying:
We are coming we are coming!
And that means fever is coming,
Village girl,
It means death will soon be here.

Let mosquitoes hum
They cannot empty my blood
With the tiny vessels they carry.

You know nothing
Village girl
Not even of *malaria*
Like a plantain stem
You'll fall one day
Not knowing why
The winds blow.

Of that city that holds your heart
Ewudu tell me more.

Oh, there are electric lights like moons
And dresses in the shop windows
The colour of sunset clouds
And then the cars to whisk you about
And dance-halls to make a peahen of you.

There's still nothing there
To tempt my steps

[54]

Two Girls Speak if there is more to tell
Of that city that holds your heart.

Oh, it would make a goddess of you
And the men devotees kneeling down before you
Your charms to ask
And you'll look at them in pity.
Lighting a cigarette you'll smile the smile of an oracle
And the smoke will scent like incense.

There's still nothing there
To tempt my steps
So leave me alone.
The canoe bears me smoothly on
Like a drop sliding on a leaf
While I fish by the riverside.
Alone in this hut
I'm worshipped by many living things
So leave me alone
I'll stay where I am
And blow this fire.

Oh village sister
In the sadness of devotion
You wait and wait and wait
While your dream is still
A solid wall without a door,
Virgin sister of the village.
Not for you the caravans of jewels
Not for you the feel of oasis water brought in pitchers
Across the desert of time.

I ask for none of those things
For what I need I have here
Life is sound
Life is sight

[55]

Two Girls Life is touch
And all the other things it is I have here
Or soon will have.
Mine are the praises of the partridges
Mine are the choirs of the cocks
At dawn;
Mine are filial memories
And I am not unhappy
While I blow this fire
And mushrooms grope for cracks in the earth
Longing for the dawn.
Ewudu leave me alone
I have this fire to blow
And fields to hoe tomorrow
Lobsters by the riverside
Mushrooms at dawn.

1961

After nearly a year of bazaars
And of the dawn voices
Of the holy men of Allah
Muezzening to the faithful
From the heights of the minarets,
And the great beach of fine sand
On which every morning
Officers of the Royal Army sweated off the fat of privilege
While formations of sea-gulls hovered
Over sinewy fishermen pulling in their trawl-nets,
And of mint tea
And writing
And seeing and listening to so many hippies being stoned
After hashish deals in backrooms
And of the djolloba-wearing and kaftaned crowds
Of the Medina and the Kasbah
And the kindness of Mohammed and Fatima
And of the other worldness of the winds of the Levant,
I ferried back to Spain
Late one afternoon
And at Algeciras got a ride with hashish smugglers
Who were transporting fifty kilos of the stuff to the
        north.
Also in the van were three Arabs
Who were going to earn a living
As gigolos at the holiday resorts of Spain
And who, considering me much travelled, sought my
        advice
On how to make money out of women
And I briefed them on Torremolinos
Where they got off
One of them saying in French
As we shook hands
That they were going to try their luck!
I hoped they'd make it
Making love to insatiable nordic blondes

[57]

The Return   For a small pay
from Tangier   While the smugglers' van headed for the heart of Spain,
The smell of hashish mixing with the smell of burning
   fuel
Which is not very different from the odour of shit.

At a small post office at La Carolina
I mailed off the ms. of a new novel to London
And we continued towards the French border
By way of Manzanares and Madrid
The setting sun blazing the glory of El Greco
In colours of gold mined by rioting gods.

Bayonne,
Montauban!
The night and the wind
And then Tours and Orleans –
Then in Paris again
And I was stone broke
And it was the smugglers who gave me a few francs
For a Métro ticket
They were white but kind-hearted;
We said good-bye
And they drove off
And I went to the Métro
Carrying my possessions with me –
A knapsack, a sleeping bag, a valise, bongo drums and my
   type-writer.
Because I couldn't afford an hotel
And I hated sleeping at people's places,
I spent the night locked up in a loo
In the Latin Quarter
Burning incense and reading the Koran
By candle-light
Until someone knocked on the door
Because they wanted to ease themselves

[58]

The Return And I transported myself and my possessions
from Tangier Burning candle included
To the stairs
Where I fell asleep until the morning.

I called on a younger brother of mine
In the afternoon
And found that he, his Spanish-born wife and children
    had moved,
Having left the place to our youngest brother
Whom I had left in Cameroon twelve years before
And who also had now come abroad.
We embraced each other.
He was very sad that I looked so poor.
I moved in with him and lived off him for a while
In that dank three-roomed apartment
Which had already been allocated to another tenant;
That meant we had only about a fortnight to be there.

A few days later
A girl smiled at me
In the rue des Ecoles
I avoided her
But she tried again
Walking right back
To pass near where I was talking to a friend
And I just had to let her pick me up.
She said she was travelling through Europe
And then she talked of restaurants because she was
    hungry
And I talked of a meal at home because I couldn't afford
    restaurants

And I wanted to make love to her.
So we went home,
My brother leaving the place for us;

[59]

The Return But after the meal and a few drinks
from Tangier And I got drunk and began talking of my new obsession
　　　　　　　　with death
　　　　　　　She absconded at dawn.

　　　　　　　My brother and I left the apartment.
　　　　　　　He went to live at a friend's
　　　　　　　And I went to live by candle-light
　　　　　　　In unused corridors
　　　　　　　Sometimes spending the night in my sleeping bag in
　　　　　　　　　alleyways
　　　　　　　Until in a round-up of layabouts
　　　　　　　One morning the Parisian police picked me up.
　　　　　　　We were driven to a prison outside Paris
　　　　　　　And in the big police van
　　　　　　　We bums called one another brothers and sisters
　　　　　　　And there was the smell of red wine and of piss
　　　　　　　And some of the sisters had bloated red faces.
　　　　　　　And one of the brothers
　　　　　　　A thin heavily-bearded man in his late forties maybe
　　　　　　　Talked all the time to himself
　　　　　　　With the haughty intensity of one
　　　　　　　Who despises human affairs.

　　　　　　　At the prison
　　　　　　　The women were separated from the men
　　　　　　　Just before we were led to the showers
　　　　　　　Where at the order of the Republic
　　　　　　　We had to wash away for a while
　　　　　　　All the moondust and stardust
　　　　　　　Of our free lives in the open
　　　　　　　And we were made to dress in Chinese-style uniforms
　　　　　　　And *sabots* for shoes.
　　　　　　　There was well-starched and ironed excrement
　　　　　　　In the pockets of my uniform

　　　　　　　[60]

The Return
from Tangier   A former prisoner must have emptied his bowels into
those pockets
Which the Police laundrymen hadn't cared to turn out
Because prisoners aren't allowed
Anything on their persons.

We were served breakfast
Then confined to collective cells
And some of the brothers were false brothers
Being clearly plain-clothes officers planted on us
To listen to whatever we said
But they paid no attention to the brother who talked to
himself
For the abundance of his words was of a world
Where the laws of man do not apply
And the soul is free to invoke night and day
In the same breath.

We were served a lunch of bread, potatoes and cattle guts,
After which we returned to the cells
And those of us who hadn't police records
Were released later in the day
And I felt wonderful carrying my sleeping bag
And copies of the left-wing newspaper
I had been selling the previous evening
And walking out of that place.
But if I should be picked up a second time
They'll put me in jail for vagrancy
Which might happen any day
Unless these poems attain on earth
The popularity I feel is theirs in the skies
Where the gods read by the light of the stars.

Most of the brothers and sisters have returned
To the Place de la Contrescarpe
And the rue de la Montagne Sainte Genevieve

[61]

The Return   And the other bum places
from Tangier Where they sit in twos or threes
Drinking red wine and despising and abusing the world.
As I come by, my hair and beard shabby and overgrown
And carrying my bag of manuscripts and newspapers
We exchange greetings and they beg
And if it is a good day I do what I can.

February 1971

B'S LETTERS B wrote the other day
From the States;
Included the Tennyson song
I sang to the winds of Aguilas
On our way to Malaga.
She writes every once in a while
Talking of San Francisco
And hoping we meet again,
And of her father
Whose wagon still rolls
In the West;
And when I was in Tangier
After I had quarrelled
With the only white liberal acquaintance I had made
In that city
Over a matter of my pride
Which I will let no one fool around with
And I was bitter against those white liberals
Who never really accept the coloured man
As their equal
In spite of instant first name civilities
And stiff upper lip friendship
It was B's letters that helped mitigate
My bitterness.
By the constancy of her tenderness
Etched against the fickle frivolity of my African girl-
  friend's
I told myself that we were all individuals
And the failings of one
Should never be blamed on a whole people.
Still I know
There is no charity in the West
And when B writes those letters
And sends me money
As she did again the other day
Knowing I am still broke,

[63]

B's Letters   I am worried
And feel I have to show her some kindness in return
Some happy day
When we are together as we were
Two years ago;
But hopes of a reunion grow dim
With the ageing of time.
With one of her letters she sent candles, incense
And a Crowley book
On the eight limbs of the Yoga
And with the candles lit
And the incense burning
I relived our friendship
And saw ourselves doing yoga exercises
By the Seine at midnight
Before we left for Spain,
While far away,
In the sunny distance of Africa,
My father was wondering
What I was doing abroad
All these years –
Just being myself, daddy,
Kissing across the colourline
Falling in and out of love
While dreaming of a black woman of home
And writing stories well into the night.

February 1971

LAKES AND FELLS *(for S in London)*

Because memory was made to reinstate the past
I still think of you
And of Holker
And our names on the walls
Of that tumble-down tractor shed
In the strawberry bush
Where we spent three autumnal days
Out there in Westmorland.

The ride from Egremont to Whitehaven
On a night of slanting rain and wind.
What is left of your memories
Of you and I in Cumberland?
Me taking over the pulpit of a village church
And preaching a sermon to you
Sitting alone in the pews?
It was raining outside
And there were graves of mountaineers
In the churchyard
And there was silence and sadness on the fells
At the evening hour
Of the rainbow fading
Over Windermere.

When I think of Ennerdale Water
And Derwent Water and of Keswick and Kendal
I wonder why I could have been seeing another face
And not you who now blaze in my memory
Like a shooting star
Too briefly-seen
And too far away
To be reclaimed.

February 1971

FROM MY Thirty centimes is all the money I have left
PARISIAN But I am full of hope without knowing why.
DIARY I laugh at the world and laugh at myself
Something of a child at thirty-five.
It has been a hard life since I ran out of cynicism
And stopped selling for a commission
Just any newspaper in the world
Deciding exclusively on pamphlets of the Left
By which I am now earning death by instalment
On a starvation diet
And the rent is long overdue.
Surely this is not a way of earning a living
Peddling slogans of a better world
In the garrison of troops armed to defend these cruel days.
But the struggle must continue
And we must open new fronts even in our dreams.

February 1971

[66]

A PARTING
OF THE WAYS
to P.A.
When a few years ago I resigned from the staff of your
    pages
I was wrong to have continued all the same writing for you
Lending to you my bitterness
Against the oppressors
And my hopes for a change,
Loading my messages on the band-wagon of our ideas
Cluttered with records of ancient ways, masks and fetishes
And manned by phrase-coiners of culture in the head
Who hum laments of the ceremonial times of the aristo-
        crats
And feudal lords of the Congo and the Senegal.
But ten years have proved
That the black colour of our skins
And a common ancestry are not enough
To hold us together
For in Africa today
The class struggle is real indeed
And I have comrades beyond the colourline
And there are black oppressors who need interminable
        elegies to the past;
And there are black oppressed and exploited who need the
        future.
I stand by the latter against the former
And out of the past I want
Only the popular dances
The arts and crafts and Swahili and a few other languages
Of our ancestors
Whom, in the cult of *griots*,
You try so hard to resurrect
When so far we have very little to show them
On this side of the day;
And so I say goodbye
As the only way out of our quarrels.
After this explanation
And a story of the river of home

A Parting of the
Ways   Not another note of mine
Near the wings of your choirs sung
To a Timbuctoo that is no more.

March 1971

A RETROSPECT And so I have sung of love
From a score of faces;
Doubts and fears and even pressures compressed
In a melody of the old times.
I have revisited the former rendezvous
I have played again with the light dreams of youth
And feel very humble
Listening alone
To the returning echo of my song.

March 1971

TEN YEARS OF EUROPE

Ten years spent in Europe!
I think of the friends I made
Some of whom I may not see again
For when we go away we rarely return
To those hearty encounters with strangers
Who later become our friends;
The men and women with whom we talked
About the past
Home and its ways
The efforts and hopes while there
And about the present
Which to many was more interesting and tempting and
    more comfortable
To talk about:
Our respective occupations
And pre-occupations –
The public ones, of course,
Or any of the creative issues which inspired
Our conversations
And shaped and reshaped our visions
Without altering the fundamental options of our past.

II And there was the refined and delicate stage-setting
Often frivolous conversations with women,
The talking and re-talking of what had been talked and
    re-talked.
And voices lingered late into the northern night
With cigarette smoke
And alcohol
In the languor of records tuned low.
And the city seeming so resolved
On leaping on to the balcony
To rip open the french windows
Part the curtains and look into the room
As if in order to referee the impending love-making
To see who wins and who loses

[70]

Ten Years of To witness the satisfaction
Europe Or the disappointment
While outside, the noise of the city rose and fell
The honking of cars,
The clatter of shoes on the pavement,
Bits of conversation,
Laughter,
The sound of cars
Racing through the night
And the opening and shutting of doors of parked cars,
While inside, in the scent of perfume and of cigarette
    smoke,
The love moments
The time of desire
The grunts and the heaving
Sometimes involuntary,
The groaning
Sometimes deliberate.
The lovely sensuality
Of perplexing excitement
Or the shallow pleasure with its hopeless nights.
And then the visits and the rendezvous,
The indifference or the affection
And then the time to part
Either because the woman was leaving the city
For another city
Or it was because the man was going with another woman
Or to another part of the world,
Or she was changing hands.
The new situations,
The new arms,
The new voices.

III But we go away and rarely return
And when we do
It is not likely to be

[71]

To the same places or to the same people.
We would find everything changed, anyway, or almost,
If we should return.
But most of the time we go away and never return
To those foreign places, faces and voices –
Unlike home which always calls us back and to which we
    return
To the traces of the past
The welcome and the eagerness to hear us talk
About our memories from abroad.

IV The happiness and sadness of those days!
The anguish, sometimes the hunger
When all funds had been spent
And one was expecting more money which delayed.
All sorts of problems.
But there were also flowers –
Those we offered in the darkness and sometimes during
    the day
And those we received in petals flattened out
In envelopes which arrived with love letters;
Our happiness with messages transmitted by passion
On exotic leaves
And all those letters written by the heart!
Oh, Etel, which was not to be –
Far away –
And the eternal summer!
But sometimes also
The shades parched up or simply disappeared
Over us
And the sky became cloudy
The winds cold
Blowing across our memories
Of the other side of the ocean.

1966–71

[72]